I AM OK WITH MY CAFÉ AU LAIT

A BOOK OF POETRY

I0544232

L. A. Davis

Absolute Author Publishing House
New Orleans, LA

I Am Ok With My Café Au Lait
Copyright © 2019
L. A. Davis

All Rights Reserved. This story is based on historical facts and is intended for educational purposes. The author recalls information from his past, and it is a recollection from his memoirs and journals. The historical documentation is contained within the public domain. No part of this book can be copied, stored, or transmitted in any method, print or electronic, without the written consent of the copyright owner.

Publisher: Absolute Author Publishing House
Editor: Dr. Melissa Caudle
Cover Designer: Ali Se
Illustrator: Ali Se
Author Photograph: Genesis Davis

Library of Congress Cataloging-In-Publication-Data
Davis, L.A.

I Am Ok With My Café Au Lait/L. A. Davis

p. cm.

ISBN: 978-1-951028-40-4

1.   Poetry 2. African American

0 1 2 3 4 5 6 7 8 9

Printed in the United States of America

DEDICATION

From the lightest of coffee to the darkest of espresso, this book is dedicated to every man, woman, and child who's been bullied, for the shade of their skin chosen for them by God himself.

Table of Contents

Introduction

Growing up on my tiny island home, I never had concerns or issues with my café au lait. My café au lait is my moniker for the color of my skin.

No one had to teach me to appreciate my café au lait; it came naturally. I never had a reason to pay much attention to the color of my skin. I never compared my skin tone to that of anyone else. As I've gotten older, I've learned to appreciate the perfect shade of my skin more with each passing year.

I saw issues with colorism as the light-skin girls were always made to feel they were prettier than the darker-skin girls, yet they couldn't be too light.

Girls with skin that was too light were called cha-cha, an offensive term. If you were very dark you were called every name in the book but a child of God.

I never heard a white person use a derogatory word to any black person on the island. They wouldn't have dared. Virgin Islanders don't tolerate such shenanigans.

Girls with long, soft, hair were favored over girls with natural hair whether long or short. If your hair was really short, it was called picky, or you were called "man head" another offensive term.

In the '70s, the afro was the in thing. Envied by those who couldn't rock one; the bigger the better. For church on Sundays "Frying," your hair was another way to wear the versatility of our crown.

It wasn't a problem because, by Sunday evening, your hair would return to its natural state from sweating. By Monday, the Afro was back.

Once the 80's came, chemical processing was the new thing. The relaxer was around for years but something called the Jheri curl put the relaxer to shame. Wearing natural hair at that time was frowned on because long, flowing, sleek hair was a must.

Who is anyone hurting and why be ashamed of what you were born with? Decades later here we are, back to where we started as the natural hair movement has taken the world by storm. I say wear your hair as you wish. We have to be our unique selves. If you're happy being "nappy" do it with confidence. If you can't achieve it, weave it, that's your right.

In many countries around this world, skin bleaching has become a phenomenon. Lighter skin appears to open doors for many, or some have a problem with the way they look because of societal pressures.

Comparing themselves to fake pictures in magazines or being scorned for being "too black," many women and men, choose to bleach their skin. Instead of loving themselves, they prefer to kill themselves for acceptance.

I've seen members of my family teased mercilessly because of the darker shade of their skin. I've never been able to understand how our race could speak about coming from Africa with its rainbow of shades yet be teased if their skin is too dark or too light. We already had to deal with that garbage from others.

I've always instilled in my children how beautiful they are. They can be whatever they want to be, go anywhere in this world they wanted to go and spend their money anywhere they decide to spend it. I know how precious and magical our melanin is. I love and take very good care of my café au lait.

This book is broken down in separate sections dealing with my café au lait, ancestry, life reflections, and to spice things up a bit, a few sultry poems just for you.

I created a recipe for café au lait for you to enjoy as you read this book. If you prefer to make it before you snuggle up, go all the way to the back. If you don't have all of the ingredients, use what you have.

The recipe can be consumed cold on those hot summer days, hot on those cold winter nights, or blended as a Frappuccino whenever you choose.

If you have your sweetheart with you, ask them to help you. The recipe was created to encourage special bonding time with the person you love. "Drink Me" would be the perfect read for you.

I Am Ok With My Café au Lait

Don't compare me to women with their long hair, long eyelashes, or eyes of every color other than my own.

Don't compare me to their light complexion or white skin. To compare me to anyone is to insult the father who created me.

God didn't make a mistake. He created a masterpiece and there is none on this earth like me.

Who told you that you are better than I? Who told you that I am less than you?

Who gave you the right to even think so? You are no better than I am because the shade of your skin is lighter or whiter than mine.

Whoever told you those things, is a liar.
Go tell them I said so! I'm fine the way I
am.

Don't you know a queen when you see
one? Don't you see the diverse ways I
wear my crown that is never crooked?

Just watch me as I walk by.
I square my shoulders, pick up my head
and sway these hips when I strut into a
room.

I don't do it to command your attention.
I don't require your affirmations.
I already know my worth.

I walk tall, to let you and the world know
that I am ok with my café au lait.

Roll With It

I do me, and you should do you.
In a world full of adversity, what else
should I do?

If you don't like the shade of your skin
that's your issue, not mine.

People may hate how you look; let them.
But why practice self-hate?
You can be the whitest of white or the
blackest of black it's fine.

Bleaching won't help you. It won't change
your DNA. Your melanin goes to deep.
No matter how much you bleach; your
melanin will seep.
It refuses to be hidden.

God crafted us for this place and time, so
I'm going to love this melanin of mine.
Move out my way.

Cause like a train on the loose, I'll run you over. Can't nobody stop me, watch me! Watch me as I embrace my melanin and roll with it.

Cursive

When I was in the first grade, I cried.
My hair wasn't as long as the other girls.
Mom told me how beautiful my hair was.

When I became a teenager, I cried.
 My stature was short.
Mom told me how beautiful my stature
was.

When I was a young lady, I walked with a
slouch. Mom told me to hold my head up,
straighten my back when I enter a room
and strut.

Now as an adult I love my natural hair
I love my short stature. I strut into a room
with confidence.

Mom told me when I wear a dress and
walk, my bum bum moves like its writing
in cursive.

Just a little darker than her, I learned to
embrace everything I thought was wrong
with me, when I looked in the faces of
others I'd see.

The Skin I'm Wrapped In

As I watch the water splash off my less
than perfect body; As the diamond water
drops cascade down my stocky framework,
I notice how beautiful my café au lait has
changed shades with the seasons of time.

I admire myself lovingly as I watch my
mirrored reflection that looks back at me. I
notice how my café au lait has soft
wrinkles around my eyes.

I examine my plump lips and radiant smile
that I flash often, and all are beautiful.

I mist my café au lait until it glistens. The
soft propellant saturated air removes all
traces as it disappears into my soft skin.

I spend time making sure my skin is as smooth as the dead calm of the Atlantic that buried the souls of our ancestors.

I have to take care of what protects me from the outside world. I moisturizer myself with long, silky strokes from face to my feet.

I appreciate how the father created me in the perfect shade of café au lait, so I make sure to take care of the skin I'm wrapped in.

His Purpose

How blessed am I to have been born in this body that didn't have to bear the scars like those before me?

I was crafted in his likeness. I'm proud of my shade. I'm proud to wear the hair I was crowned with. No excuses, no apologies, and no shame.

As I walk with pride, I allow my hips to move like running water that flows amongst the rocks, hypnotizing those who dare to stop at the banks and watch.

I meander like a stream, cool and confident in the power of its flow. I can do that because I know who I am. I know who made me.

He made sure I was crafted to his specifications, to his perfection. He made sure I was born this way to fulfill not only my purpose but his.

My Vibranium Is My Strength

My Vibranium lifts me to the highest of heights, illuminating that space around me from within.

It's the bubble in which I heal from the world after being bruised and tattered. I find my peace and grow strong and untouchable there.

This protective space allows me the time I need to search my soul so the best of me can shine through. As my healing grows, so does the space that encapsulates me.

When that space stops growing, I know it's time for me to reemerge into this chaotic world. My Vibranium is my strength.

Antennas (A protest song!)

My afro, my dreadlocks, hold hidden
secrets. They are not dreadful. Each strand
communicates with God and the universe.

My afro, my dreadlocks, hold power. Each
strand seeks knowledge.

Exploring and searching, for intuition,
wisdom, knowledge, truth, and strength.

My afro, my dreadlocks, symbolize my
reverent fear of God. They hold the
strength of Samson. My mane is the place
my prayers are stored.

My Afro, my dreadlocks, are my antennas;
the place in which the most high and I
communicate.

When I removed my mane, I severed my
mode of communication. Our
communication was sacred, and I
mourned.

With skin that looks like it's bathed in bronze, bathed in brass, or bathed in copper, my dreadlocks lay against me like a cloak of protection during war. They are only dreadful to those who see the power they behold.

My afro, my dreadlocks, are my battle dress! My Afro, my dreadlocks, are my antennas used to communicate with God.

Coffee and Chocolate

What do coffee and Chocolate have in common with human beings? Every human being fits into a shade of both.

White Chocolate, Milk Chocolate, Dark Chocolate. From light coffee to Espresso are we.

Each bean starts its life from the pores of the earth, just as we were all created. Each made to give us pleasure.

How wonderful if we all took an example from them.

I See What You Did

You can't tell me what it was like to be beaten and whipped. You can't tell me when you were born.

You can't tell me how you had to pave the way for me. How could you have known?

You couldn't tell me that one day I would have to face hate because my skin was darker than some. It's rich, bold, full of power and unlike anyone else's.

You can't tell me how you sustained yourself. How did you do it? Why did you do it? Was it due to the strength that God gave you? Was it because you knew you had to live for me?

How can I ever thank you for loving me so much that centuries apart, you would allow me to be?

Had it not been for you, I couldn't be the result of your destiny. I couldn't before, but now I see what you did. You bore the shame so I wouldn't have too. For that, I will always love you.

Aces

There are four Aces in a standard deck of fifty-two. You were chosen for me and I was chosen for you.

When bodies were bound by, love it produced my aces. They heard my heartbeat from the inside. No one else had that honor.

Could each of you hear the love song it sang from me to you? Did my heart pulsate like the sweet sounds of steel pans that sent my notes to heaven as thanks?

Did you feel the percussion of love that exuded from my being to you? What a treasure that must've been to listen too.

I envy you! I must've done something extra special in God's eye's to have been chosen to carry you.

When you stand together, your St.
Thomian and Bajan bronze shines through
you with all the culture and features that
flows within your marrow.

You're my aces today, forever, and always.
May the fruit of your loins be forever
blessed as I am to be your mother.

Privilege

I hug my children every day.

I tell them what a privilege it's been to have met them.

They smile and say thank you.

My Sister

From the time you were born, they teased you. They called you all manner of names that beat your self-esteem from your soul. The pain hurt because it was from your own.

From the lightest shade just below black to the darkest color of ebony, your own found fault in the way you were born.

If only you knew the power of your espresso colored covering, you would've laughed instead of cried.

If only you understood how beautiful and powerful your melanin is, you would've had others begging for your blessing.

If only you knew how ignorant others had to have been not to have seen the prize of the robe God himself cloaked you in from the top of your head to the tip of your toes.

Why do we bash our sisters and brothers for the shades of their skin? Why do we feel the need to use man-made instruments to change what God so richly wove together?

You are my sister and, you've grown into a beautiful educated woman, overcoming the hate shown towards you by your own and by others.

You knew there was way more to you than the words that others poured on you like scalding water.

Phoenix

I'm the phoenix who rises from the ashes of your suffering.

The fuel to my fire is the bones of the multitudes of you who were sacrificed for the ideals of wickedness.

The flames created by your bones are the hands that push me up so I can soar.

My wings spread wide to send praise to God.

I can fly because you push me from that place of my comfort. You force me to face that which frightens me.

The smoke made thick from the remnants of your frame is a sweet sacrifice to heaven.

Every vibrant color of my plumage represents the colors of every ancestor afore.

In my darkest times, my ancestors refuse to allow me to die. I hear their cheers of "Rise!"

So, resounding a sound, there's no way to ignore it.

I may die a thousand times, but the wind from the ancestors to my nostrils resurrects me.

When I feel lost, I remember the fire of their love lifting me to my highest of heights.

I'm the Phoenix born from the atrocities of my ancestors that will forever rise and soar.

My Spiritual Squad

We each have a spiritual squad. They reside in the stars as far as our eyes can see. We never see less or more than we're supposed to.

They live within the scope of our vision to ensure we stay fixed on them. They're our ancestors who twinkle a smile at each of us. The love they hold burns enough to radiate a song.

One night I was crying. Life wasn't playing fair again. I fell on my knees and asked God for help. I heard, go outside and look up to the vastness of the heavens. I obeyed and found peace.

I heard the same voice tell me the ancestors were visible tonight because they knew I needed to see them. No clouds were dancing, no rain falling. The air, cool and crisp.

The sky was so clear, it felt like I could touch the stars. There were so many, there was no way to count them. They seemed to be fighting for space to show off as they winked at me in approval.

I don't know where each ancestor came from. It didn't matter. They're all in one place now, bound to the foreverness of the heavens.

Each time I find myself losing in the unfair game of life, I look up. The vision keeps me calm.

On those cloudy nights, when I can't see the stars, I know they're there. I remember their smile. I know my ancestors and God have my back. I love my spiritual squad.

My Profile

I focused on a picture of my profile one day. For some reason, it caught my attention.

I was amazed at what I saw. The curves of my facial features showed a living scene from Mother.

My hair was a huge forest that camouflaged those who needed its protection.

I saw animals and people alike, walking from that forest to my forehead. It was an elevation, like a mountain that leads into a valley to the small hill of my nose.

I saw animals and warriors who'd traveled for miles, standing there on that hill.

They stood on the tip of my nose, hands over their eyes for shade as they sniffed the air for Adam's ale.

They found some and walked down to my lips. They were plump and full.

Water flowed from my cupids bow into the seam of my closed lips. It held a pool of crystal-clear water that flowed into it like soft ribbons.

Like finding refuge on an oasis, man and animal alike found pause. My profile hid a happy place.

No animal was afraid of man, no man was afraid of any animal. I saw warriors in commune with the animals. Both were in harmony with nature. As the winds blew a soft song, all enjoyed the coolness of the stream.

I stared at my profile again. I saw that scene like it was a mirage. I stood in disbelief, yet I was full of joy.

There stood a landscape of Mother Africa, secretly concealed in the shadow of my profile.

Welcome, Home!

I was one hundred years old.
After a day that felt like forever, the sun said
goodbye and the moon said hello. I bowed
my head in thanksgiving. The peaceful
prayer made me feel mellow.

I crawled under the covers and closed my
eyes in rest. When I woke up the next
morning, I was full of zest.

I rose out of bed. Not a creak in my step or
an ache in my bones. My vision was no
longer tinted in dull tones.

I heard music coming from my neighbor's
home. It tickled my ears. How different and
beautiful it was. I sauntered to the soft
sound. Hey, I still got it!

I prepare to face my new day. I had no desire for sustenance, so I went on my way.

 I opened the door and stepped into the fresh air. How sweetly scented it was.

The sun was vibrant almost blinding, yet I was able to see without effort. There were hues I'd never seen or had forgotten with age. I should've been frightened but I was bathing in the calmness.

I walked to my gate. My husband was standing there with a huge smile on his face. Welcome, home baby! He laughed.

Welcome home? Oh, what a wonderful dream.
Come walk with me he beckoned. We're going on a family picnic. We walked for a few minutes.
A huge table was in the middle of this gorgeous field filled with so much food it

would take a week to eat it all. Everything I loved was on that table.

Hi auntie! A soft voice said as I turned my head to acknowledge. My nieces and nephews I'd lost so many years ago were there. They laughed and yelled Welcome home auntie!

I heard my sisters and brothers. They greeted me with so much love, I wanted to melt. My dream was so beautiful I didn't want to wake up.

Hold me tight everybody! Hold me so I never wake up from this beautiful dream.

My heart was filled with sorrow with the thought I would soon wake up and be denied the incredible happiness of that moment.

You're awake they yelled! This is no dream!
We've been waiting patiently for you right
here. You took a long time.

When we knew you were coming, we
prepared this family reunion just for you.
You came home last night. Take a look to
your right.

I looked to my right and there I was, asleep
with all of my grandchildren shedding tears
of sorrow.

Oh, if they only knew how happy I was right
now, they would never shed a tear!
I asked God to send me in their dreams so
the joy I feel would bring them peace. And
he did.

Mosaic

Every negative word that entered my ear gate, stole a piece of my self-esteem. I lied to myself believing I was ok because their words didn't matter.

They came to challenge the liar in me. Each person was a shade of rich coffee. Some as black as the blackest ebony.

Dressed in beautiful intricate beading they walked me through my life. No one made a sound, no one cracked a smile.

This was serious business, and they were on a mission.

What should've taken years, took minutes but I couldn't take one step more. Just as I stopped to rest, a huge pile of broken pieces appeared in front of me. They were all different shapes and sizes.

I had no idea where that pile came from, or why it was there. It was towering.

One by one they stepped out of the huge crowd. In the deafening silence, they pointed at that pile and made me look at it.

The pile became a mirror revealing a scene where someone said something negative to me.

Each time a person stepped forward, my deepened. It was so cutting that I fell to my knees and wept.

I covered my head with the dust surrounding that pile. I wanted the pain to stop. I begged them not to make me look, but they couldn't, they wouldn't.

The last person stepped forward in silence. It was me. I picked myself up by the arm and made myself stare at that pile of pain and grief one last time.

I finally saw what that pile was. It was every negative word that I accepted as truth. Each piece was a broken piece of myself. They were the lies others said about me that I accepted as truth.

My unacknowledged pain was buried in the bottom of that pile. It represented my heaviness. The denial of my pain was the biggest lie of all.

I'd been exposed in front of this huge crowd of strangers. With my head held low in shame, I turned around to face them as they applauded in slow motion with bright smiles. Peace was immediately restored to my pain-wracked soul. Who are these people I wondered?

My twin self heard my thought and spoke. I am you; the whole you, and not the broken you. They are our ancestors. They are filled with love, healing, kindness, worth, value, repentance, humility and all the good things they know you were made of.

Like a recipe, you were mixed with all of the attributes that came from each of them. They gave a piece of themselves so that you could be created.

Now that you acknowledged your pain and accepted me, they were free to heal you from those lies.

The entire crowd disappeared into a river of gold that flowed like the rivers Pishon, Gihon, Tigris, and the Euphrates.

They flowed into that pile filling every crack fashioning the pile of pain into a mosaic of my ancestry. My twin fused with me in the flash of a vapor. It restored me to wholeness.

And then I woke up.

Let's Get Lost

Let's hide
Let's hide until
Let's hide until we
Let's hide until we get lost
Let's hide until we get lost in each other.

We won't
We won't come out
We won't come out of hiding
We won't come out of hiding until
We won't come out of hiding until love
We won't come out of hiding until love
finds us.

Raindrops

I let my robe fall from my stocky frame
gently, stepping into the steaminess of my
shower allowing the raindrops of water to
glide down my entire body like soft
diamonds.

I closed my eyes and inhaled, exhaled. I
imagined the diamonds of raindrops
removing the negativity of my day.

They followed the curvature of my body
like a map, hugging me like they didn't
want to leave.

Being forced to do so by the law of gravity
which has the last say; they moved down
the drain into the abyss of forgetfulness
taking the remnants of my day with them.

Brush

 I learned how to use it while I waited for its arrival. It was to be used to bring inner health and nourishment to my derma.

When it arrived, I held it and something wonderful happened. I saw this tool as an instrument that could be used to answer my curiosity.

I asked him to lay face down on the table I had unfolded. I took the brush from the bag assembling it according to its instructions.

The bristles even and rigid gave me the perfect reason to glide it gently across his skin. From his ankles to his entire back and neck, I moved the brush gently in a swaying motion.

A soft hum escaped his lips. I had to awaken him so he could turn on his back.

I ran this instrument in short gentle strokes up his body remembering not to miss any part of his dark chocolate sweetness.

His tone changed slightly as blood flow brought newness to his skin. The bath I ran hot for him was waiting.

Without saying a word, I guided him to the vessel where he sank into the lavender-scented suds. He almost disappeared.

I took the soft rag and rained liquid sunshine on his head. He asked me to join him but today was not about. It was all about my king. After drying him, I asked if he would lay down.

I took my warm hands, scooped up some whipped grapeseed oil, and massaged the melted gold into his pores making his skin shine like dew.

I tucked him in. He beckoned me to join him, I declined. What he needed more than me was rest.

He fell into a deep slumber. The sun kissed his face the next morning. He was a brand-new man who had been filled with love. Filled with peace. It allowed him to face the new day.

Drink Me

Yum, my husband whispered as he kissed my body from forehead to feet. He didn't stop until he got to the tip of my polished toes.

My husband adores the color of my skin. He loves it so much, he said he could taste it just by looking at me.

I look and taste like melted dark chocolate to him, and he wants to devour every bit of my goodness.

I corrected him, reminding him that the color of my skin is café au lait. He is allowed to quench his thirst by drinking from my cup of love at his leisure.

He kisses my body. Making me heat up like the sun as he loves on my silky-smooth shaved body. I feel like silk.

I touch his skin. I close my eyes to see if I could savor him. He looks like he was fashioned from a block of chocolate.

His skin has aged well with time. I caress the gray on his face that sprout from within.

We love each other in a way no one but God could understand. Our love flows like the sweetness of honey and it tasted so good.

He Always Told Me

He always told me how beautiful I was.
My café au lait, the perfect shade just so.
He kissed me lovingly as he caressed my
body with strong hands.

He took in my fragrance as he admired the
beauty of my skin. He whispered my
nickname in my ears to entice me.

He ran his hands up and down my scarred
body lovingly. He adored the cradle that
bore his seed over and over again.

As he massaged my skin to a soft shiny
glow, he reminded me of why he loves me
so.

With soft kisses all over my body, he made
me feel like I was all that mattered because
I was.

I blushed as he looked at me with love in his eyes. I allow my lashes to flutter across his face with affection.

He always told me how he loved the softness of my skin. How it gave him erotic thoughts.

He always told me.

From Your Rib

You were molded from dust and moistened with love. The clay the artist used to create you was so perfect that he didn't need a potter's wheel.

You were put to sleep for a short while and from your rib, I came.

Why did God tickle you on your side?
Because he loves a cheerful giver.
I was molded from you, for you.

We're a perfect combination. I came to relieve you of your loneliness. I came to love you. I came to stand by your side.

You were made to provide for me. You were made to protect me. My café au lait is silky and smooth as the River Nile.

When I walk, my naked hips move a smoothly as the River Euphrates.
My hair is as thick and wavy as wool, and as dark as ebony. I was made from love.
I was made from your rib!

My Her-She Kisses

My her-she-kisses are small mountains wrapped in cocoa. My peaks resemble dark chocolate syrup topped with a chocolate chip.

They always make his mouth water. As he indulges in the delicacy, the taste envelopes his mouth. I shake like a duster filled with fresh cinnamon.

As he devours my her-she-kisses I close my eyes, focusing on the multiple explosions going on in my mind and body.

My her-she-kisses melts on his warm tongue like quintessential chocolate.

How happy I am to be a woman.

How happy I am to be his.

All of My Life

I've loved you all of my life. I knew you before I ever met you because I saw you in my dreams.

I saw you with your skin as dark and hot as espresso. You filled me with warmth on those frigid nights and days whenever I thought about you.

 I knew one day I would meet you. I waited in anticipation to lavish you with all the love I have for you.

Your smile always met mine. I couldn't wait until the day I could feel the softness of your lips on my body.

Every time I saw you, you took my breath away. When I finally met you, I knew you were the one I had been waiting for all of my life.

I was patient. You were worth the wait. I never doubted your love because you had already shown it to me.

Your Love

Your love feels like the ocean on a warm day. Your waves of love make me feel nurtured.

Your love crashes into my heart like waves against rocks. Its' music is so sweet to my soul that it makes me want to dance by myself.

I've never met anyone like you. When you're not around, I feel empty.

I miss you when I close my eyes at night, even though you're sleeping next to me.

The moment I laid eyes on you, I saw my future and it was beautiful.

I had to have you, for such a gift is only given to us once in a lifetime.

Q and A

Q. Who are you and why are you here sir?
A. I'm your destiny, my love. I'm here because
you prayed for me.

Q. Don't you remember your prayers?
A. I've prayed many a prayer, sir.

Q. You asked God to pick your mate, didn't you?
A. Yes, I did.

Q. Where did you come from sir?
A. I came from heaven.

Q. Are you soft in the head?
A. No, but challenge me my love.

Q. Ok, who sent you?
A. El Elyon, El Roi, El Shaddai, Jah, Jehovah
Jireh, Jehovah-Rapha, Jehovah Shalom sent me to
you my love.

Q. Why did he send you?
A. Because I chose you to be my helpmeet.

Q. Why did you choose me to be your helpmeet?
A. God sent your prayers to me and I listened.

Q. What did you hear?
A. I heard my desires recited back to me from your lips. I heard my voice. Everything I asked God for, you requested in your petitions.

Q. Do you believe me now my love?
A. No, sir for you didn't tell me what I said.

Q. Did you not ask God to send you the man he has for you and not the one you want?
A. Yes, I did, for I no longer trust my judgment sir.

Q. Do you believe me now my love?
A. Yes sir, I do. I accept the gift that God has granted me through my prayers.

Fortunate

What did I do to have met you?

What prayer did I use as intercession before bedtime for you to be gifted to me?

What dream did I have that could've made you appear silently in my life?

What wish did I make in my times of quiet that could've made you manifest in my space?

What part of heaven did you reside before God decided to send you to me?

What did I do to receive such a blessing as to have met someone as wonderful as you?

The answers don't matter.

Even though you weren't in my life for long, I was beyond fortunate to have met you.

The short time spent with you is worth every thorn prick that goes through my heart when I think about you.

I would endure the pain over and over again if just to have another moment to love you.

You never had the chance to taste my café au lait, nor did I have the chance to stir yours but the love we carried within has left my heart filled with gratitude for the special time we shared.

Tears (Call)

Every tear we shed contains a word, a phrase, a message.

I've shed many over you.

I'm afraid to awaken from my dream each night. The dream that contains you and me.

I love you so much I can smell the sweet aroma of it.

You didn't know love had a scent, did you?

It smells exotic like agarwood that burns in silence and it looks like you.

Each time I meet you in my dreams and have to say goodbye, I wake up with tears streaming down my face that touch my beard.

They stream down my lips, past my chin, and like icicles, they drip on my barren chest.

The chest that holds your head in rest.

The chest where my heart beats for only you.

The chest that you run your fingers across and compliment because of its dark shade.

As I hold your face, like a book I read each of your tears.

They say, don't leave me, I love you, I'll miss you, I need you, I hope to see you again.

I say goodbye waking up to face another day where I daydream of when the sun sets so that we can meet again, and I smile.

Sunset (Answer)

I wake up with my eyes filled with tears after saying goodbye to you in my dreams.

My tears give me joy in the morning as I have the entire day to anticipate seeing you when I close my eyes each night.

Knowing that I'll meet you in my dreams gives this woman all the fuel she needs.

I've never seen a man crafted in such perfection.

Your skin is as smooth as freshly spun silk and as silky as satin dyed in the perfect shade of brown.

It looks like God poured you in to your perfection.

Just thinking of holding your hand as we walked through grass that shines in the sun like jewels help to make each day perfect.

I can't wait to wrap my hands around yours.

I have so much to tell you when I see you again.

I look forward to the setting of the sun each day so we can meet in that secret place in our minds.

Wait there for me my love; I won't be too long. I'm coming to find you at sunset.

In-to-me-see (Intimacy)

What do you see when you look at me?
What do you see when you talk to me?

When you lay your head against my brawny chest. Can you hear what my heart says as it pulsates with love for you?

Whisper to me what it says. I want to feel your warmth when you whisper it in my ear.

When we spend time in quiet conversation can you see into me? Can you understand the meaning behind my words?

What am I saying?

Can you in-to-me-see?
I see into you.

I can see how much you love me by the way you look at me.

I can see what you think of me with each smile and by the way, your eyes shine when you see me for the first time each day.

It would make a man out of any boy if anyone looked at them the way you look at me.

Your skin looks like café au lait speckled with gold dust. Your kisses taste just as sweet.

You've managed to conquer me at the deepest level; a place within me that I never knew existed.

Lady you have made me feel things I've never felt before and it was worth the wait.

Lazy

Your friends can't stand me.
They call me lazy.
Filled with fury, they ask, what kind of
man would sit in a car and allow his wife
to walk into an establishment
unaccompanied while I sit in the car and
watch?

I can assure you, my love, I'm no lazy
man. I'm your protector, the guardian of
your existence.

Your friends have no idea how much I
love to sit back and watch the way your
body moves when you walk.

They have no idea of the pride I feel to call
you my wife.

They have no idea how I feel when people stand aside to let you enter and exit the room like a queen entering and exiting her court.

They have no idea how I admire the way the sun glistens against your beautiful, dark, skin.

They have no idea of the anticipation I feel when I see you walking towards me.

Yes baby, let them call me lazy. They have no idea what they're talking about.

No lazy man could ever think of doing the things I want to do to you when we're alone my queen.

Search My Heart Word List

AFRICA

MUCHYOUMEANTOME

ANDYOU

NEVERBEA

DESIRE

OFMYHEART

FROMTHEDUSTOFF

SEARCHTHELAMP

GENIE

TENDERLYWITH

GRANTYOUEVERY

THEONEWHOWILL

IAMHERTOHONOR

TORUBME

IATHE

WAITINGFORYOUR

IFYOUTHINKIT

WILLSEEHOW

ITWILL

YOURLOVERRELEASE

IWILLDOIT

YOUWHOHASMADE

LIMITOFTHREE

Search My Heart

```
N G G X R L                         M A H F P T
  C C J N X O P Q S                 B F P Q J T C E Y
  M V U D W X Y E E  T F            B L R F A R E J  Z T Q
 O K G J M J X J A A Z E K          A P O W F N M T F R B I  E
U O Y D N A U A R T B T Z H         A J V A I S O H R R U A S U T
 O M U N Y X O C U L U E J U G      Y S N D S T E O X S E A R F D
L J F G U J G H T L C F Z U Q X J   C U D T K N O M D X B B O E R U H
E K B G E T T W B Z H Y L H Z I F F U C G O X A N T G B R O N V J E G P
T M U Q K H O B S H V J C G P D E S I R E G Q E E H V C E M O K P U I U W
U E M E E R H T F O T I M I L D D K C F G D M W E K U V Y H K N E E D G X
S E F L Q O A P D M Q L R R F E V F N Y J U H D G N E N O Y W I C K S O T
X B A J D K L V W C A P E M B U R O T G O O U E M N Y T G C X E I I F Y X
E M Y E C I I F Y O U T H I N K I T A Y W S N U H O E C Q T P Z T M O H I
P G W K H A T E N D E R L Y W I T H H I T I U A U R T F Z K N W Y U W L T
K H B R H M L Z C L K I L D T G S C L O E Q X W E M S V K R I H R R W U X
 I K W V T R A X X G J P R G L U L F N A W H H S I T M Q L E L E Z A R
 T Z E C H E L W Y V H E W P M A Y G Y O O M T P V Z F L A O U J H W Y
 Q C D E E V A X R K P G C U A K T K X H A Q J I O J H R V G H E Q K P
 Q Q G A T V T N Z Y E D G N K C S A I T W Y O O Y T E P B B K O R
 Y U O Y R O F G N I T I A W Y K S P K A L X A F D R G P B N D U N
  X C J C H J Y X P U H Y F R M Y F L A E V P V E L S O V O S L
  E X A F R I C A A R Q T F A B B E V A H V X L N Q L A V V X O
   J L O F U X T S Z Y G D E V J R Y J Q M E G X Z W I K W D
   F X K W C K I M U F E Q Z J A O M Y U A J C K A S U W K T
    D Y M J R D K F E J N T V J K L P S M K G O F Z F L I
     T P W O H E E S L L I W Q N D E Q C L O T Z C P B
     D H U S B R C P L V Y R E V E U O Y T N A R G H X
      Y G A R R E H Q C F K P J Q D E W H F A Q O Q
       R E S B B U P W P N T V F M L E N F I E G
       Q U Q S R D X G O Q Y M B P C V Q M M
        Y P U U Q D L X U X E I Y E C R I
         I V A E L K Y F O R C B F O D
          D V B A I L B M K R K B G
           A T X H R P Z E P Q A
            V N W U M O T E Y
             U J Y V U O E
              F D L U A
               R P Z
                B
```

Search My Heart

Search the lamp of my heart and you will see how much you mean to me.

I am the genie waiting for you to rub me tenderly with your love.

Release the one who will grant you every desire.

It will never be a limit of three.

If you think it, I will do it.

I am here to honor you who was made from the dust of Africa.

A Letter To My Little Self

Never listen, believe, or accept the
negative words of others. Especially from
those who were supposed to protect you.

You are not worthless.
You are worthy.

You are not ugly.
You are beautiful.

You are not fat.
You are perfect the way you are.

You are not dumb.
You are intelligent.

You won't amount to anything.
You will create witty inventions.

You won't do anything.
You will do great things.

You have no friends.
You are loved by many.

You are evil
You are kind.

I should've given you away.
You are wanted by many.

Have confidence in yourself.

I Apologize

When I was a child, I thought as a child.
Maturity has chased that child away.

I wanted to be one of the boys, so I joined
in when the other boys teased you because
your hair was "nappy" and your skin was so
dark.

More than thirty years have passed, and I
can still remember the look on your face
when I teased you mercilessly.

The sadness in your eyes has been painted
in my memory like a haunting that won't
give me rest.

I am ashamed of that little boy.
I knew better, I was raised better, I was a
bully.

I didn't realize the princess you were, nor the prince I was.

Both of us, from a strong people.

You were my sister even though we didn't come from the same mother or father.

I should have protected you.

Left by the death of my queen, I became a single father, forced to deal with my harshness, through the eyes of my daughter.

I see you in her.

I see how she wears her crowning glory that I once made fun of through you.

She cares for her crown with pride.

I wonder if you took the same pride in your crown only to have it bent by the blow of my words.

Wherever you are, I want you to know that I love you.

You are my sister.

For everything I said to hurt you.

For everything I did to make you shed tears.

For everything I said to strip you of your self-worth, I apologize.

Sprinkled

I was feeling exceptionally lonely one day. I was weeping in despair, reflecting on all of the hurt I had poured on so many in my younger days.

All the tears I saw shed over me without concern or care. All the love that was given to me that I ignored. The shattered hearts I was responsible for.

My neck bowed with face in hand, I shed my tears as my body jerked. For so long I wanted this moment.

Fear of me never being able to stop the torrent of tears filled my heart so I never did.

I calmed myself after my emotional release. I was able to look outside of myself. This time the view was beyond beautiful.

I was sitting, looking out of a window. Everything was as blank as a canvas. No color, no sounds, no shapes.

I watched as a hand came down from heaven right above my window pane. The hand extended three fingers.

They were shiny as new bronze and moved smoothly, rhythmically, making a beautiful high-pitched sound like when a zephyr wind blows through wind chimes.

The fingers began to sprinkle the earth with a brown sugar-like snowfall that sparkled in the sun like amber.

I watch in awestruck silence as you were being created. It took hours but I couldn't move or take my eyes away.

There was never a moment when those fingers stopped moving until you were a beautifully finished work.

After the final crystal fell, the fingers snapped with a loud thunderous sound.

Like a beautiful song, created by the wind, you came to be.

You walked towards me with a smile.

You wiped my tears and hugged me leaving a sugary smear on my being.

It glistened like sunlight on a still body of water.

You told me you were all the love I had discarded earlier in my life and had prayed that would come back after years of penitence.

You told me you were sent to heal me from my guilt.

Each time I cried, you wiped my tears leaving a sugary sweet streak of yourself on my face.

You sacrificed yourself for me as you melted each time, I shed a tear. You left your mark on me, filling me with sweetness, kindness, love, and forgiveness.

One day you were no longer here. I didn't need you anymore. Your destiny was fulfilled. I've been restored; made whole because of you.

On the Wings of My Prayers (call)

You were the best things that ever happened to me. Why couldn't I see it?

I thought I was an adult. I didn't want to hear your words of wisdom. I didn't want to hear the love that was hidden in your nagging.

You are both gone now, and I feel like an orphan. I wish you were here. I would give a year of my life to each of you, just to hear your voices again.

I stand here a man wishing I could take back every word that shattered your heart, and to dry the invisible tears I made you both shed.

I forgot how hard you worked to make sure I had what I needed.

I forgot how mom stayed up all night when I was sick.

I forgot how you made sure I never saw a hungry day when you went without so that I wouldn't have too.

I couldn't accept that I couldn't have the things everyone else had.

I was selfish and even though you never said it, I know I brought you much shame. I can't imagine how sad I made you.

I am sending my sorry on the wings of my prayers and I hope they reach you.

Yellow Butterfly (Answer)

My child, we have received your prayers. They were delivered to us on angel's wings. They were so beautiful.

Why are you wasting your precious time in guilt over your past? We're enjoying our new life while we prepare a place for you.

We live in a land of such beauty there is no way to describe it. Colors and music, unheard of.

Rivers made of diamonds that flow in four directions from a mansion of gold so large, that the biggest mountain on earth can never compare.

Singing as you've never heard all day and all night. The sun never goes down here. There is no need for sleep.

We are here with all of your ancestors. They are too many to count but all are beautiful.

From those with yellow hair, pale skin and eyes which couldn't bear the sun, to the blackest of ebony skin tone are here.

We forgive you and we forgive ourselves for the mistakes we made.

In the time you have been praying we have been sending you signs. You couldn't see it because your heart was burdened, and your head low.

Lift it and look at the sky.

The yellow butterfly is our love and assurance that we received your prayers and we are ok. Rest now and forever receive the gift of forgiveness.

I Am Already Complete! (Call)

How dare you enter my space with your chest fanned out in defiance and speaking to me with disrespect!

Who do you think you're talking too with such disdain? How long have you known me to think you can speak to me with such contempt?

I've shown you love when no one else would. When you couldn't stand yourself, I was here to love you.

I was here to uplift and dig out the treasure hidden deep within your weary soul. No one else but God and I could see what was hidden there; not even you!

You brought your broken spirit to me and I saw far beyond it. I never tried to change you. I loved you exactly the way you were sent to me. All I did was love you.

How dare you round your lips and release those words from your tongue against me? How dare you say without you I'm incomplete?

Bitch, please!

I'm the woman that saw no flaws in you when there was plenty to speak about.

When you had nothing, I was here.
When you felt like nothing, I was here.

I saw strength in you when you couldn't see it in yourself. I hid your shame when you spoke your deepest secrets to me in the darkness of the night.

No one else but God and the weeping angels could hear them.

Every night, I let you touch my body.

I polished your crown so that when I placed it on your head before you walked out that door each day, people could see it shining in the sun against your dark tone.

They went together perfectly. The bright light your crown emitted hid your troubled soul. I was the most blessed woman.

You were the most blessed man only you were too arrogant to see it.

When I was just a thought in God's mind, I was already complete.

When I was placed in my mother's womb, I was already complete.

When I entered the bright lights and cold air of this cruel new world, I was already complete.

When I was given to you, I was already complete.

Even now, after you've been made whole, after crushing my heart by deciding to leave, I remain complete.

I heard my ancestors laughing when those words fell from your lips and entered the ether.

I can still hear them laughing. They said, "I got you girl!" In all of your ingratitude, I still love you.

In all of your bitterness, I still love you. The door is open, you may go. Take whatever you need with you.

I give you my love and best wishes, but I will never give you my dignity.

Never forget that I never needed you, nor anyone else to complete me.

I'm already complete and because of it, I am the woman I am, and you are the man you are today.

In More Ways Than One (Answer).

I was wrong for speaking to you with disrespect, defiance, disdain, and contempt.

I never had anyone love me the way you loved me. You loved me even when I couldn't stand myself.

You never spoke anything but uplifting words to me. When my soul was weary, you gave me respite.

I couldn't see the treasure God hid in you; the woman he masterfully created for me. Worse; I had no idea of the treasure he hid in me.

I was a broken man that no one else but you wanted. You accepted me exactly the way I was. You saw no flaws in me.

My broken manhood was my Karma for the selfishness I'd shown to so many for far too long. Your love was my redemption.

When I had nothing, you were here.

When I felt like nothing, the winds of your love made my wings spread to its limit. It allowed me to soar.

You saw strength in me I couldn't see in myself.

I didn't know you went into your secret place to intercede for me.

I didn't know you were polishing my crown. I didn't know I had one.

I didn't know you put that crown on my head before I left the house each day.

I didn't know you made sure it was straight. All I knew was each day I woke up in your arms and I was happy. I knew when I walked out that door, I was a new man.

I never put a crown on your head, yet you never complained. You continued to love me.

Your love gave me strength.

I had no right to say such bitter words.

I had no right to say that without me, you were incomplete. That was a lie and the reason why my life is now so disenchanting.

I spoke into the atmosphere what I felt about myself.
You told me that you didn't need me to be complete because you were already complete.

You told me I didn't need anyone to complete me because I was already complete.

Even with those beautiful words, I couldn't see in myself what you saw in me.

Well, my love, I might be complete, but my life without you isn't.

You hid my shame and my darkest fears when I held you in the night.

In our time alone where only God and the angels could hear; you held me.

In the chambers of your heart, you still hold my secrets.

The scent and softness of your warmth in the darkness made me feel like a King.

I was blessed to have the queen of my dreams next to me. In your arms, I was strong.

I couldn't wait to come home at night to see you. I couldn't wait to hear your voice during the day.

I missed you every second I was away from you. In all of my ingratitude, you loved me.

In all of my bitterness, you still loved me. The moment I stepped out of that door and heard the click of that lock, I regretted it.

Too full of pride to admit my regret, I lost my dignity, while you kept yours.

You said your ancestors were laughing when I said without me your life is incomplete. I didn't hear them and thought you had lost your mind.

By allowing those words to slip by my lips, I offended God, you, and your ancestors. I can hear them laughing at me now. Their laughter haunts me. It's brought me to your doorstep to ask for your forgiveness.

The crown you polished in secret is now my mirror. I had to search my soul to find out where I went wrong.

I'm the same cycle of self-centered, and selfish person I've always been. It's caused me the loss of many a love.

The difference is, for the first time in my life, I care about the woman I've lost.

I've lost the best thing that's ever happened to me. You're already complete in more ways than one.

Precipice

Life plays for keeps. It will give you everything
your heart desires, then snatch it away just as
quickly.

I've found myself standing on the edge of a
precipice.

I've prepared to jump many times.

Depression consumed my soul. You said you'd
always love me, and that memory kept saving me.

I don't know how you knew.
When I prepared to jump, your voice always
spoke, "I love you."

Maybe it was all in my mind.

I never treated your right. I didn't consider the
damage I was causing. Your smile hid the
bleeding lacerations I marked on your soul.

I thought you'd always be here for me.
You finally found the courage to leave.
I was broken when you did.

I never tried to regain you. I knew I had done too much. You had enough. I had worn out my welcome.

Of all the women I savored, it was only your voice I heard in my anguish.

When I prepared to jump in an attempt to leave this dark place.
When I prepared to meet my fate, it was your love that kept me here.

Maybe I was right after all. You've always been here for me.

It was your voice that saved me.
It was your love that kept me alive.
I thought life was finished with me.
I was finished with life and I wanted no more of it.
I thought life had been cruel to me, but I was the cruel one.

The pain I reaped on you was undeserved. You saved me, and in doing so, showed me that life is worth living.

Life without you has been difficult. I accept the consequences of my actions.

I wonder if that man knows how lucky he is to have you? I was lucky to have you love me.

Because I experienced unconditional love, my life has been made better.

I stand at the edge of the precipice today. Instead of wanting to jump, I use it as my footstool to show how tall I am.

Not her loss

When a man hurts a good woman, the best medication to begin the healing process is her ability to identify her value.

Once she realizes her value, she will be able to gather up the broken pieces and use the healing power of faith as the glue to seal those open spaces.

When those spaces are bound, she will understand that the loss was not hers but his.

Love (Call)

You can't love anything on this earth without the
promise of eventually losing it.
Love always ends in pain, yet loving and being
loved is worth it.

Pain (Answer)

I've seen the grief of many.
I never gave it a thought.
The shade of the person's skin didn't matter.
Compassion has no age, range, or color.

To make the person feel better I'd say things like
"God wanted the person back", or *"they're in a better place."* Those words filled the awkward space of not knowing what to say.

Once the person was in the ground, that was where it ended for me.

I went back to my daily routine with the thought of the person passing briefly in my mind and nothing more.

Karma has a way of catching up with our words and actions. I finally had to face personal grief.

It was so deep I would've gladly chosen death instead.

Just like me who tried to show empathy, I found people trying to give kind but hollow words.

They were filled with explanations about why it happened.

The person devoid of understanding didn't see how their rationale was causing pain.

It was my friend, my family member, my child, my father, my mother.

They still had their friend, their family member, their child, their father, their mother.

What did they know about my pain, or why it happened? Not a darn thing!

Death is a debt owed, and we must pay. It won't be forgiven in seven years or removed from our credit report if we don't pay what's due.

There's no compromising the price; no way to decrease the amount to settle it.

Like a woman who screams in pain when we bring forth life, we must all deal with the pain of death.

If someone has passed and you don't know what to say, simply tell them "I'm sorry for your loss," and leave it there.

Love always ends in pain, and your hollow words heap on sorrow.

Runners

I ran from my demons.
Sometimes it was in slow motion.
Sometimes at Olympic speed.

My demons were patient.
They kept chasing me.
They ran in a pack, at the same pace
At the same distance.
They never tired, but I did. Others were smarter.

They sat in the spot where I left them. Filing their talons of hate, they waited patiently for my expected return.

With the full expectation of me coming back, they waited to rip me to shreds with a smirk on their face.

Each time I went back to face them, my exhaustion turned to bravery. I pulled out my sword of the spirit.

When the battle was joined, my sword cut to the heart, leaving my demons wounded. I left them behind in the place where they were defeated, and I never looked back.

Move by faith

I learned to remove my eyes from my problems.
I focus on helping others in their time of need.

My fear of being rejected by others, whose skin
shade was different from mine was an issue, but
still, I moved.

When the person in need swallowed their pride.
My offer of help was accepted.

It allowed God the freedom to fix both of our
issues without human logic, human will, or human
interference.

Therein I learned to move by faith.

Forgiveness

How easy it is to withhold forgiveness
from others until we need forgiveness
ourselves.

Tit for Tat

What I don't know might not hurt me, but your vindictive spite will hurt you.

You hold on to that secret betrayal, waiting for the perfect time to unleash it.

Dirty secrets are a burden to the soul
It rots you from the inside out.
There's no need for me to posture for a war of tit for tat.

My positive energy is as precious as Black Opal and Red Beryl. I have no desire to waste it.

The universe knows what she's doing. That destructive secret of betrayal you're holding in your arsenal.

Yes, the one in which you intend to smite me with at my weakest, will get heavier when your secret and karma converge.

Gossip

I loved to gossip. The juicier the better.

It felt good slipping off my tongue. It felt even better when it slipped off the tongues of others.

As the information entered my ear gate and engorged my soul with the venom of those being gossiped about, it filled me with climactic pleasure until the day the gossip was about me.

Gossip is a dark, toxic, sludge to the soul.
To the soul of the person doing it.
To the souls of those listening to it.
To the soul of the unsuspecting victim.

Indulging in gossip murders the innocent.
We bring judgment on the person; we bring judgment on ourselves.

The universe hears every word and she never forgets. Her clockwork and timing are aligned with precision. She will render her judgment accordingly with perfection.

The contents of my dark heart and soul were exposed. I showed those around me, I was the starter of strife; I showed others, I was never to be trusted.

Extinguishing the fire of the gossiping tongue quickly! Run swiftly from those who indulge at its table. Look at the person boldly and say *That is none of my business*. It's the only reply you need.

It will leave the gossiper off guard.
It will leave the offender with a cloak of shame.
It will make the offender powerless.
It will allow bad karma to escape you.

The Firsts

After the grief of loss
The first year is the worst
We have to deal with every holiday, every special
moment. I call it "the firsts."

The first year to adjust to our new normal.
The first year to accept what our hearts can't
reconcile.
The first year to make peace with the outcome.
The first year to discover when we will find our
smile.

No matter your color or creed. The first is a dark
place where we don't pray but plead. Plead to the
powers that be to take the pain away. You get past
the firsts and discover you'll be ok.

L.A. Davis's Café au Lait for two

In this last section, I created my version of a café au lait. This recipe can be used to create some bonding time with the people you choose to make it with. I tested it with my daughter, granddaughter, and daughter in law. We had a wonderful time making and testing it.

The prep time for this recipe is twenty-four hours since you will need the ice cubes and cold utensils.

Making your café au lait will take minutes if you prep everything in advance. I hope you enjoy making it with the person you love, which is you.

4 cups whole milk
1 Vanilla bean
2 Cinnamon sticks
2 cups coffee beans or fresh ground coffee (you may opt for instant coffee)
1 Bottle of caramel syrup (or coffee syrup of your choice)
2 Coffee cups or mugs
1 small saucepan

1 wooden spoon
1 cup of heavy whipping cream (optional)
1 electric mixer
1tblsp powdered sugar
1tsp instant coffee
2 metal bowls (one large, one small)
Ice cubes
Dash of cinnamon powder (optional)

Grind two cups of coffee beans or purchase a bag of fresh ground coffee beans. Brew a fresh strong pot for this recipe. If all you have is instant coffee, use it.

Another option is using a French press. Pour ground coffee in your press, add hot water, let steep as you make the hot milk.

In a saucepan, add four cups of whole milk and 1 cinnamon stick to infuse. Stir until hot. **Do not boil**.

Cut open a vanilla pod. Scrape a small amount of seeds from the pod and place it at the bottom of an empty coffee cup or mug.

If you can't scrape the seeds, cut a small piece of the vanilla pod and put it at the bottom of your cup. As the pod softens, you may see vanilla seeds rise to the top of your café au Lait so don't panic.

Remove cinnamon stick for the milk and add to cup or mug. Pour hot, fresh brewed or instant coffee and heated milk in each cup simultaneously.

Add flavored syrup to your taste in the café au Lait. Top with homemade whipped cream (optional) and stir with the cinnamon stick. Dust with cinnamon if you'd like.

L.A. Davis's iced Café au Lait for two

If you desire an iced café au Lait, after brewing your coffee, add vanilla seeds, or a piece of the dried pod to your hot coffee. Add 1 cinnamon stick to infuse and allow the mixture to cool to room temperature.

Once cooled, remove the vanilla pod and cinnamon stick. Pour some of this coffee mixture into an ice tray and allow it to freeze hard.

Place 3-4 coffee ice cubes in a glass.
Pour cold milk and the remainder of the cooled coffee into the glass simultaneously. Add syrup of your choice to taste. Add plain or coffee whipped cream, dust with cinnamon powder (optional), and indulge.

Top and front view of iced Café au Lait with Cinnamon and Vanilla Bean infused Coffee ice cubes.

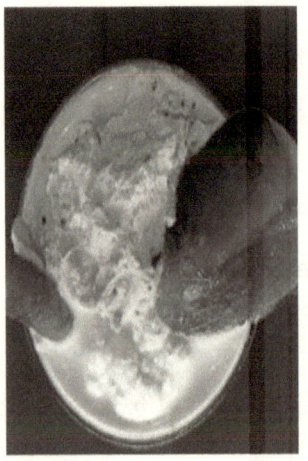 

L.A. Davis's Café au Lait Frappuccino for two

8-10 Coffee ice cubes
2 Cups brewed coffee that has been infused with vanilla and cinnamon stick (cooled)
2 Cups cold milk
Add flavored syrup to your desired taste
Dash of Cinnamon powder (optional)

Pour all ingredients into a blender. Blend to desired smoothness. Pour into a glass, top with plain, or Coffee whipped cream, and dust with cinnamon powder if you choose.

Top and front sides of Café' au Lait Frappuccino

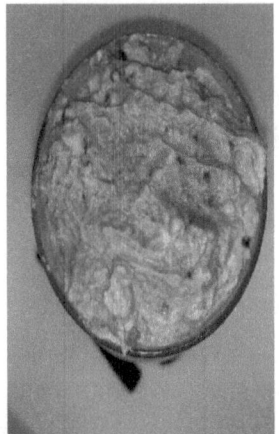

Plain and Coffee Whipped Cream

1 small metal bowl
1 larger metal bowl
1 electric mixer
1 cup cold heavy whipping cream
1-2 tablespoon powdered sugar.
1 tsp instant coffee; add more if you desire
stronger coffee flavor.

Freeze metal bowls and metal beaters from the
electric mixer overnight. (The colder the bowls, the
faster the whipped cream will form.) **Remove
bowl from the freezer only when ready to use.**

In the bigger metal bowl, add regular ice cubes.
Sit the smaller bowl on top of ice cubes.
Add ice cubes around the smaller bowl to keep
cold.
Add 1 cup of heaving whipping cream and 1-2
tablespoon powdered sugar to the smaller bowl.

Beat the mixture on high speed until soft peaks
form.

Take one half of this mixture and set aside.

With the other half of the whipped cream, add instant coffee to your desired taste.

Whip until the coffee is incorporated. **Do not overbeat this mixture.**

Whipped cream can be used to top the hot café au Lait, iced café au Lait or Frappuccino.

All recipes are best when served with someone you love, or while snuggled up under a blanket with this book. Whipped cream can be made in advance and stored in a plastic bag or container for a few days. Let me know how you like it.

The End…For now!

About the Author

L.A. Davis earned her Doctorate of Education with an Emphasis in Organizational Development. She was born on the island of St. Thomas and is a member of Zeta Phi Beta  Sorority, Incorporated. She has written four books and is currently working on a coloring book series for children.

So, You Want to Be A Doctoral Learner Huh? Are You Nuts?!

Where Are My Children?!

When I kiss Em, They Stay kissed

I Am Ok with My Café Au Lait

Contact Information

Dr. L. A. Davis
2403 W Stan Schlueter Loop #690923
Killeen, Texas 76549
Davislad2018@gmail.com

www.ingramcontent.com/pod-product-compliance
Lightning Source LLC
Chambersburg PA
CBHW052207170626
46812CB00004B/1685